MY VIEWS ON GRIEF

DR. A. JOHN PRADEEP EBENEZER

Copyright © Dr. A. John Pradeep Ebenezer
All Rights Reserved.

This book has been published with all efforts taken to make the material error-free after the consent of the author. However, the author and the publisher do not assume and hereby disclaim any liability to any party for any loss, damage, or disruption caused by errors or omissions, whether such errors or omissions result from negligence, accident, or any other cause.

While every effort has been made to avoid any mistake or omission, this publication is being sold on the condition and understanding that neither the author nor the publishers or printers would be liable in any manner to any person by reason of any mistake or omission in this publication or for any action taken or omitted to be taken or advice rendered or accepted on the basis of this work. For any defect in printing or binding the publishers will be liable only to replace the defective copy by another copy of this work then available.

This Book is dedicated to all the families who are in utmost grief. The pain of losing the loved one is excruciating if it happens suddenly and unexpectedly. We lost our son Master J.Allen Albert on 16th, October, 2021. He was 8 years old. Almost One year without him was a daunting life for us. All the statements and quotes were the feeling we felt when our little Allen left us. We are there for you. We know and we have experienced that nothing can comfort but a sense of being connected with families who are now experiencing grief gives a slight relief. Eager to meet our loved ones in Heaven.

Contents

Preface

The pain my family going through for the past year, since we lost our 8-year-old son has been unbearable. Every second in our life passes in grief. When we started experiencing grief, we didn't know how to get over it, we also didn't know whether our thoughts were right. We had and we have many unanswered questions too. This Book summarizes the experience we are encountering daily and what we have learned about grief. We hope that this book brings comfort to your doorsteps.

Acknowledgements

My sincere thank you to God Almighty who has Strengthened me all through these years. I also thank my son Master J. Allen Albert who has shown me how to lead a perfect life, in his short stint for 8 years in this world. The Character he possessed was something unthinkable and divine.

ONE

GRIEF

1. GOD becomes the number one enemy if you have really loved HIM.
2. Tears are no more a visitor, Stays forever.

ϸϸϸ

3. Scars longing not to be erased.
4. Wish every new dawn is a doomsday.
5. Wish Heaven is not a fairytale.

ϸϸϸ

6. Smiling always becomes a fake.
7. Only one question in my mind, why?
8. Wishing what had happened was a dream.

ϸϸϸ

9. Happiness is a Sin
10. Festivals and Celebrations become a two-edged sword
11. Guilt becomes the first thought every morning.

ϸϸϸ

12. A sense of Selfishness often crosses the mind.
13. Sleep Hypnosis doesn't work.
14. Purposeless footprints.

ᚦᚦᚦ

15. Pain up to the throat.
16. Places once cherished become deserted.
17. Intense longing for the Hugs and Kisses from the invisible

ᚦᚦᚦ

18. Death becomes a Cake Walk.
19. Birthdays become Saudade.
20. Grief Bacon becomes a reality.

ᚦᚦᚦ

21. Many say Time is a healer, No, as time rolls by grief increases.
22. Graveyard seems a nice place to sleep
23. Feels like a hammer hitting the chest.

ᚦᚦᚦ

24. Life becomes cruel
25. Mind searches for the person who is in grief and longs to be a part of it.

TWO

GOD TO WRESTLE WITH TEARS

1. GOD becomes the number one enemy if you have really loved HIM

Grief is an inconsolable state in which we hardly get comforting statements from fellow friends and near and dear ones. For a person who has loved God and put his or her entire trust in HIM losing a loved one means, a war is going to break out with God. Grief, because of an untimely death of the near and dear ones initiates a fury with God. Conversation between us and God will go on till we reach eternity.

My Take: There is nothing wrong in getting furious with God at the time of Grief, who else we can rely on? God is there with whom we can fight.

2. Tears are no more a visitor, Stays forever

For an actor to cry, glycerin is needed. For a person who is experiencing grief, tears are no more a visitor it stays forever. Hearing a song liked by the lost one, seeing a face like the lost one on the roadside, and visiting a place where we usually spend time brings tears. More horrible is continuing to live in the house we often cherished, even the sight of the walls brings tears.

My Take: There is nothing wrong with crying, it brings us close to the taken ones.

❧❧❧

THREE

SCARS, DOOMSDAY, HEAVEN

3. Scars longing not to be erased

Grief brings an indelible scar all over the body. What is amazing is, the mind wishes that the scars are not erased. Scars bring out the feeling of being heart to heart with the taken loved ones. Every new day leaves a unique scar.

My Take: Scars are the invisible tattoos that the mind long for.

ᗞᗞᗞ

4. Wish every new dawn is a doomsday

Grief treats doomsday like a child's play. Wishing a great fire from the sky, why not today become the God-fixed rapture date, different thoughts cross the mind while getting up from bed. Nuclear war or a bioengineered pandemic is not a distant probability to happen in the near future, doomsday can very soon be a reality.

My Take: Doomsday is the Birthdays for the grieving ones!

ᗕᗕᗕ

5. Wish Heaven is not a fairytale

A grieving mind wishes Abou Ben Adhem's poem a reality. As the lines in the poem depict "The next night the angel came again with a great wakening light and showed the names who love of God had blest, and lo! Ben Adhem's name led all the rest", the grieving mind longs that heaven is a reality and their name should lead the rest.

My Take: Longing for Heaven to be a reality cross the mind every second, Grieving mind long to be a part of it to meet the loved one.

ᗕᗕᗕ

FOUR

FAKE SMILE, WHY?, WISH IT WAS A DREAM

6. Smiling always becomes a fake

As the words of Stanley Gordon West go "Smile and the world smile with you, cry and you cry alone." a grieving person always has a fake smile on their lips to make the world smile with them. That smile says a thousand stories.

My Take: A grieving Heart smiles with a crying heart.

ᗡᗡᗡ

7. Only one question in my mind, why?

Normally the unthinkable, unbearable happens to Godly ones. So it is not strange for a grieving person to ask Why? God Why? If not With God then with whom?

My Take: The answer doesn't arrive, but still Life has to move on.

ᗡᗡᗡ

8. Wishing what had happened was a dream

Every day a grieving person wakes up with the notion what had happened was a dream. It is the only time the feeling of happiness crosses the mind like a mirage, sadly it doesn't last long and a feeling of disappointment crushes the heart.

My Take: A Grieving person wishes to lead a life in dreams.

ԾԾԾ

FIVE

SIN, TWO-EDGED SWORD AND GUILT

9. Happiness is a Sin

In grief, we move to a state that happiness is a sinful activity. Function, exhibitions, and going to shopping malls, and cultural centers are boondoggle activities. A grieving person sees that happiness doesn't enter their heart.

My Take: A grieving Heart Cleanses itself.

ϷϷϷ

10. Festivals and Celebrations become a two-edged sword

An invitation to a function, festivals, and celebrations tends to pierce the heart. Anger as an outburst is expressed on the person enjoying the festivals and celebrations.

My Take: A grieving Heart often feels like a sword pierced it.

ϷϷϷ

11. Guilt becomes the first thought every morning

Each and every activity of a grieving heart has a sense of guilt. A feeling of shame or regret creates excruciating pain.

My Take: Guilt isn't necessarily bad. Sometimes it's even productive.

SIX

SENSE OF SELFISHNESS, SLEEP DEPRIVED AND AIMLESS WALK

12. A sense of Selfishness often crosses the mind

A Sense which makes us think we've been very selfish. A thought of we've been mainly Self-centered and let go of our loved ones from this world. Day to Day activities like a morning meal, or a special lunch will create a thought of selfishness in the mind, that our loved ones are not here to eat.

My Take: A thought of being selfish kills us. It's challenging to apologize, but once you do, you feel a tremendous feeling of relief.

ᗱᗱᗱ

13. Sleep Hypnosis doesn't work

Grief causes a state of inadequate quantity or quality of sleep, including voluntary or involuntary sleeplessness. Almost Every Clock striking after an hour is heard. Grief makes us awake always remembering the loved one who has slept forever.

My Take: The Eternal Sleep of our loved one keep us awake.

ᛈᛈᛈ

14. Purposeless footprints

A grieved person leaves purposeless footprints wherever they go. Almost all the things they do becomes customary. Grief makes the legs head out the door without any agenda.

My Take: I wish I had no footprints. My soul with yours. Waiting for that day.

ᛈᛈᛈ

SEVEN

EXCRUCIATING PAIN, DESERTED PLACE, HUGS AND KISSES

15. Pain up to the throat

The skin becomes hot, we develop a large lump in our throat, and the eyes start to water. We attempt to swallow or clear our throat, but the tears only start to come. Some can Experience a lump in their throat that lasts for weeks at times of high stress. This happens because of immense grief due to the death of the loved one.

My Take: A lump in the throat, only a bereaved family can understand

ϼϼϼ

16. Places once cherished become deserted

You can feel isolated and out of place in your town or culture as you and your family attempt to get through the holiday season. But you're not alone. The voids created by death in their own family circles are acutely felt by many people in your immediate vicinity. Finding new ways to get through the holidays is a challenge shared by all bereaved families.

My Take: Holidays will get deserted, it is gut-wrenching

ᛈᛈᛈ

17. Intense longing for the Hugs and Kisses from the invisible

Longing for the Hugs and Kisses which will never happen brings agonizing pain in the heart. The imprint left by the kisses on the cheek longs to be everlasting.

My Take: Longing for the Hugs and Kisses from the invisible is a heart-wrenching wish that we know it will never happen.

ᛈᛈᛈ

EIGHT

DEATH, SAUDADE, GRIEF BACON

18. Death becomes a Cake Walk

The fear of death takes a back seat when we are in grief. Anytime, Anywhere the mind is ready to face death, it becomes a cakewalk.

My Take: The pleasure of meeting the lost one takes the front seat

19. Birthdays become Saudade

Birthdays bring a deep emotional state, a longing for happiness that has passed, or perhaps never even existed.

My Take: Wish our birthday, the lost ones birthday never cross the mind

20. Grief Bacon becomes a reality

Real grief makes us gain excess weight that results from binge eating because of sadness, despair, bereavement, or any emotional condition.

My Take: Gaining weight in grief tells about the sadness hidden inside

NINE

TIME, GRAVEYARD, HAMMER HITTING THE CHEST

21. Many say Time is a healer, No, as time rolls by grief increases

The longest and hardest stage of mourning is typically depression. Ironically, it's eventually allowing ourselves to feel our greatest sadness that lifts us out of depression. We eventually reach a point when we can accept the loss, give it some meaning in our lives, and then move on.

My Take: Grief stays on till we attain angel wings. The last breath of ours takes the grief away. We open our eyes in eternity joining hands with our loved ones.

ϷϷϷ

22. Graveyard seems a nice place to sleep

The best places to focus on the truths of life and death have always been cemeteries. When visiting a cemetery, many people have a stronger sense of kinship with God, and their deceased loved ones.

My Take: A Sleep in the graveyard brings a sense of closeness with the lost one

❧❧❧

23. Feels like a hammer hitting the chest

Intense sadness can change the heart muscle to the point where it results in "broken heart syndrome", a heart condition with symptoms that a hammer is hitting the chest.

My Take: Life without that intense pain increases the guilt feeling

❧❧❧

TEN

CRUEL, FAMILIARIZING THE UNFAMILIAR

24. Life becomes cruel

Sometimes life becomes cruel and it has its own way of putting us in the trash. Finding our way out can be challenging, and getting back to feeling normal might feel like a battle for days. A feeling of lack of interest or giving up arises because you feel defeated can result from being knocked down.

My Take: Life is definitely cruel when a father buries his child

ꝑꝑꝑ

25. Mind searches for the person who is in grief and longs to be a part of it

If a grieving buddy doesn't want to chat, sit with them if they do and pay attention to what they have to say. Be present and offer a judgment-free environment so they can express their emotions.

My Take: Just sit and cry with a grieving person, it means a lot to them

ϷϷϷ

ELEVEN

QUOTES ON GRIEF BY GREAT PERSONALITIES

1. Grief is the price we pay for love.

-Queen Elizabeth II

ᗞᗞᗞ

2. Given a choice between grief and nothing, I'd choose grief.

-William Faulkner

ᗞᗞᗞ

3. If tears could build a stairway, and memories a lane, I'd walk right up to Heaven and bring you home again

-Author Unknown

ᗞᗞᗞ

4. Grief is like a moving river, it's always changing. I would say in some ways it just gets worse. It's just that the more

time that passes, the more you miss someone.

-Michelle Williams

ϸϸϸ

5. Tears water our growth.

-William Shakespeare

ϸϸϸ

6. Without you in my arms, I feel an emptiness in my soul. I find myself searching the crowds for your face - I know it's an impossibility, but I cannot help myself.

-Nicholas Sparks 'Message In A Bottle'

ϸϸϸ

7. It's so curious: one can resist tears and 'behave' very well in the hardest hours of grief. But then someone makes you a friendly sign behind a window, or one notices that a flower that was in bud only yesterday has suddenly blossomed, or a letter slips from a drawer... and everything collapses.

-Colette

ϸϸϸ

8. The melody that the loved one played upon the piano of your life will never be played quite that way again, but we must not close the keyboard and allow the instrument to gather dust. We must seek out other artists of the spirit, new friends who gradually will help us to find the road to life again, who will walk the road with us.

-Joshua Loth Liebman

ϸϸϸ

9. Those things that hurt instruct.

-Benjamin Franklin

❤❤❤

10. The best and most beautiful things in the world cannot be seen or even touched. They must be felt with the heart.

-Helen Keller

❤❤❤

www.ingramcontent.com/pod-product-compliance
Lightning Source LLC
Chambersburg PA
CBHW021156130726
47988CB00004B/1634